The
Poems
That
Grief
Wrote

The Poems That Grief Wrote

Ronnie Brenner

ASTORIA BOOKS

Copyright © 2024, Ronnie Brenner

All rights reserved. No part of this publication may be reproduced, distributed, or transmitted in any form or by any means, including photocopying, recording, digital scanning, or other electronic or mechanical methods, without the prior written permission of the publisher, except in the case of brief quotations embodied in critical reviews and certain other noncommercial uses permitted by copyright law. For permission requests, please address Astoria Books.

Published 2024
Printed in the United States of America
Hardcover ISBN: 978-1-7364605-4-2
Paperback ISBN: 978-1-7364605-5-9
E-ISBN: 978-1-7364605-6-6
Library of Congress Control Number: 2023922696

Astoria Books
Seattle, WA
info@astoriabooks.com

Book design by Stacey Aaronson

Names and identifying characteristics have been changed to protect the privacy of certain individuals.

*I dedicate this collection of poems to my beautiful daughter,
Jen Birmingham*

*It was her encouragement, then insistence over the years,
that brought these very personal poems to daylight.*

Contents

Note to Reader ... 1

Cancelled ... 3
Laying on Hands ... 5
Guidelines for the Anti-Cancer Diet ... 7
Gene ... 9
The Ottoman ... 11
A Mounting Threat ... 15
To Eat or Go Blind ... 17
Panic ... 21
Dr Gisella Perl ... 23
The Art Dealer ... 25
The Hot Dog ... 27
The Kiss ... 29
I Love My Furry Legs ... 31
A Fart ... 33
Back from Katrina ... 35
Lyla ... 37
No Drinking ... 41
The Artist's Son ... 43
She Wasn't Packing ... 45
The Inspirational Speaker ... 47
Chloe and Akio ... 49
Liposarcoma ... 51
Cloud Jumper ... 53

Alafair at 3 ... 55

My Love's Nose ... 57

Transfusion ... 59

He's Leaving ... 61

Orchids at 2100 ... 63

A Green Death ... 65

Unsure ... 67

Bro ... 69

I Watched You Dance Today ... 71

A Miracle ... 73

No More Poems ... 75

No More Poems #2 ... 77

Note to Reader

These poems, in essence, delivered themselves during the course of my husband's dying, sometimes waking me to write one in the wee hours. Some follow the painful path of losing him and are witness to his love of life and my love of him. Others describe earlier events, revived by this emotional journey. Maybe surprisingly, some have a clearly comical theme, or have humor stippled within. While they were born of grief, because humor was always present in both our lives, playful poems are interspersed with serious ones.

Different sorts of loss are represented, including those that are by-products of rejection, familial cutoffs, emotional abuse, and neglect. These experiences can be devastating. Their negative imprint on a young child can be indelible. Anxiety and self-doubt are the focus of two poems.

Some recount the love and, often, loss of other people and pets. One tells of the aftermath of Hurricane Katrina, and the near loss of a city and the horrendous loss of many of its people. Another describes a hypothetical "inspirational" speaker and his duplicitous life—raising the subject of trust. Two sequential ones describe the experience of severe physical pain one night, followed by one of joyful gardening in the morning.

Humor does pop up in unexpected places. Noticing the comical in life, especially in the midst of adversity, has buoyed me and thankfully accompanied me throughout my life, even in my role of therapist. My patients and I, while taking problems very seriously, could often lighten a heavy load.

One poem laughs at the utter confusion in trying to provide an anti-cancer diet, another the role of farts in the family system, of a hot dog in a farewell. One tells of the excitement in observing an exuberant young grandchild. The one about furry legs arrives when, after a span of wee-hours writing, I feel and see the rising sun shining on those legs. One tells of a grandma's double bind, relative to food. A note, scribbled on a shuttered building, triggers a rather musical one. I believe these particular poems came to me as occasional and welcome "poetic relief" from sadness.

I hope you'll join me on this journey.

CANCELLED

flashing white bursts into the room
entourage in tow
hello
she begins

she projects the scan
the surgeon as disgusted football coach
the patient as errant player

too late too big she barks
sorry
she exits

huddled together so tight so small
nails into flesh
sobbing
holding
we exit

Laying on Hands

It began one evening before I asked if it was okay
and once done, he asked that I continue.

Creaming my hands with Jergens,
I try to soften them and capture
the almond cherry memory of his bubby,
as I make an untrained reach for the ancestors.

He stretches out before me,
baring the torso I've loved and known so long.
The uninvited guests that bulge
remind me there's a medical story,
but it's just a detail now.

My eyes close, as do his; my hands rotate gently,
firmly up and down his belly and chest.

God bless my wonderful man.
God heal my wonderful man.

Sneaking a sign of the cross, I intersect the vertical
with an occasional horizontal path.

And so continues this swirling, spirits-seeking,
nonsectarian mutual trance,
until finally I rest my hands
on the two prominent bulges
and we are both very still.

I kiss his belly.
He sighs.
I love you, we both say,
and kiss lips then cheeks
goodnight.

Guidelines for the Anti-Cancer Diet

Eat only dark skinned grapes
even if you're branded a grapeist racist.

Don't make things dark.
For God's sake DON'T CARAMELIZE!
It might kill you even if you're dying.

Pick fruits and veggies so brilliantly colored
that you could accessorize with them.

Eschew the "conventional"
though you know the contrasting label
should read "highly imaginative"
or "avant-garde."

Be warned that red beets juiced with carrots can
mimic a hemorrhage and vault you to the hospital

Study your grains, nuts, and berries
for two hours at Whole Foods.

Act like you intended to buy
ten pounds of pucca berries
when the lever runs away with you.

Master the art of writing on a quarter inch twist tie,
understanding that the i.d. could end up lost in the twist,
like in the sixties.

Fail at grain and you might
unwittingly sprinkle raw farro
on your crucifers or corrupt
your pudding with flaxseed

Make, bake, and store your granola
for centuries in, you know, air tight containers.

Ask some questions aloud or in your head:
How do they milk the almonds?
Does hemp ice cream demand a coverup?

Know that cheese substitutes can
make you really really sad.

Embrace chickens that dance with farmers,
not chickens that hang out in multi-family housing

Do cows that eat grass, not cows that do drugs

It's a dangerous organic world out there.
Tread lightly.

Gene

The scent of geraniums, not the scented ones,
the common ones, transports me
to that loamy place where Gene lived.
Nature himself, I thought.

Every plant in my grandparents' garden
was settled there or germinated by him
in their glass house.

In those reflecting rooms,
we made cuttings of geraniums
and nestled them in boxed beds of moist sand,
next to the carnations, one of those selected
by Grandpa each morning for his lapel.

Surrounded, as we sometimes were,
by musky bulbs underground in the musty root cellar,
I recall once asking him to show himself.
I know he never did,
nor made me feel ashamed that I asked.

In his old truck he shared his lunch with me.
A child as hungry for his provisions as were his cultivars.
I could have eaten anything in Grandma's kitchen.

He, the German refugee, not Jewish,
and soon after the big war,
made me swoon with giddy pleasure when
he opened his round-topped lunchbox
and then the waxed paper to the intoxicating smells of
I don't remember what glorious sandwich.
We just shared it, the two of us, such buddies.
Even the chunk of milk chocolate,
he carved into two pieces with his pocket knife.

Sheltering the koi fish from the harsh winter,
he brought them into the glass house.
He did the same for me.

Tended by him, I grew to be a decent gardener.
I wish I could show him the brimming pot
of scarlet and pink geraniums
boasting in my living room today,
grown from cuttings smelling just like him.

The Ottoman

I was so small when I made my first impression
on the tufted stool in my parents' bedroom.
Like children's heights,
whose marks are known and shown on walls,
the age and times I sat there
are held more in the memory of the ottoman,
than in me.

The elegant prop that was the seat
for my mother's dressing table,
hijacked by my father,
became the one of his tyranny,
specially reserved for me.
Detained there,
I learned of all the crimes of my young life.
There they were counted, codified, and archived.
One of them comes to light:

I heard Buddy whimpering and, yes, screaming
and caught sight of Dad dragging him by the collar
along our endless driveway to teach him a lesson
about running after cars.
Clumsily fighting for traction on the smooth paving,
our princely dog, now brought to his knees,
his dignity dissolving in the dripping pee
etched by his paws, he cries for help.

Please, Daddy, don't hurt him.
It was involuntary, uncontainable,
like the promise of retribution
that captured my father's face.
Shunning was always his first penalty of choice,
not a word addressed to me for weeks and more
until the grim summons to the ottoman.

You're a disgrace, a worthless snip of a child.
You'll never learn.
Don't look at the clock.
Look at me.
I can't say I remember the rest because
I think it slipped into the ottoman,
while I watched,
with the volume down,
the grimacing, pacing, wringing of hands,
despising of me.
Just like clockwork, the two hours passed.
He was spent, and I could return.

Get out of here, he ordered, *you snip of a child*,
he said again, raising his leg to kick my bottom,
never making contact, as if to say,
even my foot is wasted on you.
No violent man . . .
it was widely known,
he would never strike a child.

Witnesses, there were two:
my mother, silent, draped across the bed,
propped up on one elbow,
and my little sister,
hiding in her closet,
a vicarious captive,
hearing against her will.

Your father was a great man, many said at his funeral.

A Mounting Threat

Even now, I would only peek at them on Nat Geo
or Wikipedia through semi-spread fingers.

Sea monsters, still as sleep, encircling me,
each with one eye walled, the other set on me.

A bitty girl, no more than five,
told by her to just stay here.
Sit there.
Fear-frozen, I had no wanderlust.

Remember Uncle George?
she asked before she left me there.
No cousin's dad,

He and she slipped away
for much more time than I could count,
leaving me in the care of a petrified nanny
with a sword for a nose.

To Eat or Go Blind

The coconut cake, did you have some? Five layers.
The coconut's fresh. The frosting is to die for.
Your grandfather's having a rest. He played 9 holes.
A lot of men at the club still play 18.
There's no reason to change his routine.

You have such a beautiful face;
if only you watched what you ate.

I'm liquiding. It's wonderful, every Wednesday, nothing but
clear broth and tea. I have so many luncheons and parties,
I have to mind what I eat.
Try this. It's the best chocolate you ever put to your lips.
It's Ida Mae. I bought five pounds of it.

Don't eat so many of those; try the nova from Max.
Don't wear that top. It makes you look fat.
Ten pounds would do the trick.
Gene put out the azaleas. Have you seen them?
These carnations are all from him.

Share this delicious sandwich with me. It's pastrami.
I love the coleslaw and pickles. I always ask for pickles the
minute I sit down—watermelon rind, green tomatoes,
piccalilli, it doesn't matter what kind.
These are the best potato pancakes ever.
No one makes them like Marge, crispy, with sour cream.
Lean over. Just take a bite.

The boys are playing in a tournament.
If they win today, then two more times,
I think they'll take the cup.
I just bumped into Lillian, a perfect size 2. She's gorgeous.
Someone should scoop her up.

You've never, in your life, tasted anything like this.
The caterer made it just for me—a carrot ring.
It's coated with crushed cornflakes.
Did you ever hear of such a thing?
People say I have the best parties. I always love to dance.
But if your grandfather died, God forbid,
I'd never dance again.

You're eating like there's no tomorrow.
I'm always watching myself.
I'll just give this a wrap or two and put it back in the fridge.
You're not eating. What's wrong?
I can't have this going to waste.

James, would you tuck me in in the back?
Can you see any bulges?
Make sure you've smoothed them away.

Ina stopped by—such a lovely woman, a perfect 6,
maybe sometimes an 8. All the men are crazy about her.
Who wouldn't be? Though she doesn't have your face.
How can you still be hungry? Just a minute ago you ate.

Your mother's been on a diet, taking those pills to lose weight.
They're all the colors of the rainbow, you know,
the ones in that plastic case.
She sees that doctor what's-his-name.
That's all he does all day.
Her mood is so up. She's never been happier or thinner.
I think she wants to take you too, maybe even your sister.

We're eating very soon.
Just taste this. You don't want to spoil your dinner.

Panic (1967)

Making a left on Lex at 34th,
nothing dramatic in that—
when an invisible behemoth from nowhere
bashed me in the chest.

Taking my air with him,
he disappeared straight off.
I made one failed attempt to catch the breath,
but not the thief who made off.

Tingling toes and fingers, strap molasses legs,
vision unreliable, seeking a saving face,
heart rushing before a tornado—
Is this the way I end?

A doorway to a frame shop,
a quasi-known nice man.
False-composed, I enter;
too ashamed to say that, by the way,
I think I've lost my mind.

The concocted guardian nearby,
the breath again my own,
I'm grateful for the respite from what's been going on.
Reviewing on the sly, predicting against my will,
straining to comprehend the scary movie
I'm shocked to know I'm in.

Dr Gisella Perl

She had laughing/crying eyes
like that actress Maria Schell.
Beautiful happy to see you ones
that shifted to haunted ones full of pain.
I made a note of it.
She examined me and those incredible eyes
told me I was fine.
Years later, when I returned to her,
the pained eyes were in charge.
She didn't like what she found—
a tumor the size of a football.
Benign, but it tore me up inside—
twenty plus procedures.
I was able to have a baby girl,
and her eyes were joyful that time.

Then appeared a syndicated story
about a prisoner/doctor,
a movie not far behind.
Auschwitz, I learned,
was where her eyes were primed,
under the tyranny of Dr. Mengele.
My doctor Gisella Perl was imprisoned there.
She was directed by Dr. Death,
just hours after she arrived, to gather a thousand
pregnant women to take to a more agreeable site.

He exterminated the lot of them,
leaving Gisella horrified,
her sense of complicity always on her mind.
The rest of her tortured stay,
with only a rock and her bare hands,
under cover of night,
she performed abortions to attempt
to preserve more women's lives.

I received a letter from Dr. Perl around 1979.
She wrote that she was closing her
New York practice in a few months time.
She wanted to finish out her days in Israel,
delivering as many Jewish babies as she could,
to atone for those lost young lives.
That is where she died.
I know that as she welcomed
each child into the world,
those laughing eyes presided.

The Art Dealer

When I had a gallery in the 70s,
I sat for hours at a rolltop desk
with a whippet's wet nose on my foot.
She was Ursula of Ursulines,
in deference to our street.
Fine prints and other works on paper sounded lofty;
in truth, I spent a lot of hours sitting by myself.

From time to time, a critic would pop in and say,
"Great show!"
I was rewarded with choice reviews,
had a few dozen happy collectors, and a number
of local artists who rarely missed a show.
But, more often, a chatty head would appear and ask,
"Hey lady, you do all these yourself?"

One day a woman asked, "Do you have any Katz?"
This was to be an auspicious day,
heralding the arrival of a discerning guest.
With pride, I produced a self-portrait
and an exceptional profile of Ada.
"NO! CATS!" she protested, "kittens in particular."

Adding insult to esthetic injury, the confident,
not competent, fellow next door sold offsets
of duck paintings for $400 a pop,
with customers queuing up.

How banal to purchase a reproduction
in lieu of the genuine thing.
Still, I assumed it unwise that I
don a sandwich board defining original print.

Ursula would give it a different spin.
At noon she ambled down Toulouse to Chartres
and the famous Cafe Banquette.
Unfamiliar with her breed,
they thought her a starving dog,
and daily fed her a monster burger
on a crusty French baguette.

I knew it was time
to work by appointment from home,
when a man took a leak inside my front door,
and announced he was coming to get me.
Ursula, turning attack dog
(probably from all that beef protein),
stood equidistant between him and me,
spinning and gnashing her teeth.

One look at her, and he ran like hell.
I looked and was stunned by her heart.
The event punctuated the end of my stay
on Toulouse at Ronnie Brenner Fine Arts.
That skinny girl saved my life
and my love of art,
and never held over my head,
the loss of a damn good meal.

The Hot Dog

She was dying
She called for her children
One at a time
For no long visit, she said,
Just a quick goodbye

She suddenly asked for a hot dog
Having almost stopped eating at all
I leapt to the task wholeheartedly
A last wish I'd hope to recall

I had to make it perfect
This final exchange
A hot dog to please the Gods
So excited this opportunity came

Knowing her taste,
I butterflied and grilled it
In the center Velveeta
A warm toasted bun
That would crown the visit

Whipped some cream for Jello
Wanted to utterly please her
A rose from the garden, the final
Procedure

She cried when she saw it
I cried too
Finally bonding over Max's Deli
That was decidedly new

"I wasn't the mother you needed,"
She surprisingly said
The first time a comment like that
"It was all fine," was my sendoff
Because I felt I could live with that

The Kiss

It's bewildering this game of
who can you trust? It's hard to both
honor and reconcile the must.
I have memories of kindness,
but it's often short-lived.
Honor thy father and thy mother.
Is that my default?
Just condone and forgive?

Ambivalence here can prove problematic.
Take this event of which I often think;
Albeit a bit on the side of dramatic,
It crystallizes the conflict of which I speak:

When mother lay in her coffin,
I had an impulse to kiss her cheek.
Then freaked as I lowered my head,
afraid she'd open her eyes and ask,
"What do you think you're doing?"

Like heading down a slippery slope,
there was no turning back.
And *basium interruptus* seemed a
piteous way to act.

So I kissed her cold left cheek,
then quickly lifted my head.
My fears were clearly unwarranted.
No sign of a blink to dread.

I Love My Furry Legs

I love my little furry legs
though I know I'm not supposed to.

It feels so rebellious, primal, downright outlawish—
my secret inside my pant legs.

Yes, I know they ought to be foamed
and Gilletted, with blades
specially curved like my curvy self.

But when the early sunlight shines
on those girlish curls,
I'm just so
proud of myself.

A Fart

A fart is a gift a loving family gives itself.
A resounding truth from the gut.
Game of whodunit,
rousing uproarious laughter,
measured in degrees of stink or loudness
and quality of sound.
Detonating explosive.
Rumbling distant train.
Tumbling small rock slide.
Whispering bubble in a bath.
In polite society, a fart is to be feared.
Embarrassment of limitless range.
Harbinger of unwelcome events.
Latent escapee to be restrained at all cost
lest it slip out, or worse, thunder out,
sullying one's reputation forever,
to say nothing of one's underwear.
When permission is given
throughout the system to fart,
it invites harmony.
Promises there is no aspect
of any member that is unwelcome.
In response to a fart,
one might feign annoyance
or feel genuine disgust.

But in the end, or out of it,
a fart is the ultimate
visceral primordial expression
of something deep within.

Back from Katrina

A young rookie cop, a rookie no longer,
stood guard by the bar near the door.
Watching over his charge, he was focused on them.
No one appeared to be noticing him.

All around robust hugging, cheers of reunion,
rattling trays, clinking glasses. No one toasting him.
In partial shadow, his sweet face apparent,
his weapon in view at his side.
Close enough to his childhood,
it didn't take effort to imagine
his young version playing cop.

His story was silent, just there for the asking.
He was here for the nightmare, the city at war.
A kid from a small town far from New Orleans.
One could only imagine what images seared
through his soul:

People stranded, looters shooting up streets,
boats trolling down roads turned to water,
people and pets pleading and crying for help,
first responders steering through bodies afloat,
finally hauling them in.

Someone approached him, started asking him questions:
Had he slept? Did he need an air mattress? Had he eaten
warm meals? Were the hot humid nights too oppressive?
Did he have a place to bathe? Did he have any siblings, a
significant other? His mother must really be proud.

At the end of the meeting, he shyly asked for a hug.
The listener freely embraced the young hero and
thanked him for all that he'd done.
A quiet exchange had been transacted,
and only two in the whole crowd had known.

LYLA

We left her there in the dark hallway,
no windows near—
our four-inch conure with the six-inch tail,
in a cage to suit a portly chihuahua,
bowls to sustain a retriever.
We didn't have a clue.

Two days max was our routine. Not now.
Desperate in Houston, we watched on TV—
waters rising, people stranded,
floating bodies, houses washing away.
Mixed with grief for our city
was blame for our bird.
Such horror we couldn't foresee.

Lyla, our screecher, interruptor of phone calls,
gourmand of diverse wooden objects,
laughter impersonator, prankster,
diminutive dental hygienist; competitively, no contest.
She inhabited our hearts and our scariest thoughts.

Rarely given to disturbing fantasies,
Joe dreamed all our rear windows blew out of the house,
and a snake had eaten her whole.
When I heard that narrative from this calm guy,
my heart was hard to console.

Once before, we almost lost her
when a backfiring car launched her high in the air.
Surprised, she made a right on Fourth,
a left on Camp, leaving not a trace.
Five hours I sobbed and walked the streets,
calling her name, and incredibly found her safe.

Too many weeks were passing; the city remained closed.
Then appeared a young cop from home,
checking on his folks. He made his way to Lyla,
fed and watered her and gave us a call.
Cheered, yes, but she still remained in the hall.

A tryst with our friend the brain surgeon
was her second rendezvous.
Had she been a writing conure,
she could have told of her handsome protectors
in some sort of online review.

Finally, a quick pass allowed—
we found her none for the worse,
bathed her in bottled water
and left her old cage on the curb.

We took her with us to Breaux Bridge,
only thinking ahead, while our neighbors,
eyeing that poopy, feathered cage,
sent condolences, assuming her dead.

Home for good, we had her for two more years.
She died during a home manicure.

The young man performing it was traumatized,
as it was not his usual experience.
But the manicure was not really
the cause of death—just age and maybe stress.

Of course, memories of her are still with us,
picturing her miniscule self,
seated between two full-sized adults,
noshing a wedge of Theo's pizza,
looking so pleased with herself.

NO, DRINKING
NO, ALCOHOLIC BEVERAGES ALOUD
ON THIS PROPERTY

*(the above note scrawled on a
shuttered building)*

The guy from the next block over,
who's giving his best friend the horns,
knows nothing would blow his cover more,
than his beverages turning to song.

No one wants to hear rowdy booze.
We came here for tacos and beer;
not to suffer Dos drunken Equis slurring
our mariachi favorites off key.

Prosecco has those neat little bubbles.
A little juice helps keep it calm.
If those bubbles get overexcited—
they could break the surface in farts.

So please keep your aqua vitae sub rosa.
We don't want them calling the cops.
It reflects on you when your beverages
whoop it up in a public place,
so gag them as soon as they start.

The Artist's Son

He failed to guard the vessel
And you were emptied out
Like surplus slip
From a model never cast

Precious boy, dark eyes and hair
Jubilant little one

He left and didn't return
His absence framing
Your own reflection
The palette diluted
Colors muted by disregard

Precious boy, dark eyes and hair
Sadder then

Your right of passage—finding him.
No sweat. Address well known

And there he was but vaguely limned
Soft words alone would fill you in
His anger came instead

Precious boy, dark eyes and hair
Accomplished man; still anger flares

Please know and guard this truth
For life—If he had had
That missing piece, some bas relief,
It would have gone like this:

Precious boy, I am so so sorry
I let you down
I was so wrong
There's no excuse
I love you and won't leave again
Forgive me, precious boy,
My long awaited son

She Wasn't Packing

She wasn't packing a gun,
switchblade, or totenschlager,
just the declaration,
"I never want to see or hear from you again."

Easily rankled or pissed,
she seized the opportunity
to put me on the do not contact list.

One false move and I was definitely out.
One word, ineptly filling in the blank said,
"no more chances,"
and me with no awareness
of edging closer to the brink.

She died during the "we're finished" years
and only her son broke his silence, not hers—
"It was colorectal cancer,"

But it felt like suicide,
because the voiceless taunt remained—
"Ha ha! I got to leave this world
never speaking to you again."

The Inspirational Speaker

The inspirational speaker told his wife
to get off her fat ass and ask herself
what she was getting out of being a pig,
said she was a disgrace.

The inspirational speaker asked his son
when the hell he would learn to
squeeze from the end of the tube,
and slammed him against the shower door.

The inspirational speaker hooked up
with a woman who'd silently wept
through his most recent gig,
then said she was pitiful,
that she'd better pull herself together and get out.

The inspirational speaker glided across the stage
to roars and applause, grinning broadly.
When the folks sat down from the standing ovation,
he began with the topic at hand—
BEING YOUR AUTHENTIC SELF.

(No one I know, but we can't always know.)

Chloe and Akio

Old friends at one time wed, now
He lay across the foot of her bed
Rightly so; she left decades ago
Their lives had taken other forms

Advancing night led him naturally
From perpendicular to parallel
Coming to rest on the other half
Honor bound, respectfully unattached

Lying side near side in partial sleep
Dozing and waking at partial peace
He raised his arm to encircle her dog,
In purest love, in surrogate form

Liposarcoma

surging
inflating
crowding him out
weighing him down

supple skin now taut with
your greedy brutal bulk
riding roughshod
forcing him into history

no way to overpower you
get you out
beat you up
one-up

you are stealing him away
wrenching him from me
restricting my detesting you
as part of him

I am feeling the loss of him coming as
this chilling season leaves me shivering
anticipating his constant warmth
withdrawn

Cloud Jumper

I asked him what was the thing
he feared most about dying.
He said he knew it didn't make sense
and it wasn't fear.
It was sadness that, once gone,
he would be missing me
forever through time.

I said we must have a meeting place
where we can be together any time.
I looked out the window from the bed
where we'd just held each other crying.
A fluffy white cloud, I said,
and he responded, cloud nine.

I asked how we would know which one.
He said all the clouds are numbered.
In the end, I said
It will be in any and all clouds I'll find you.
You will be the Cloud Jumper.

Alafair at 3

Rock star convert and improv songster;
owner of a shiny blue guitar.

Diminutive soccer gal, stretching her arm to
encircle her teammate in a burst of camaraderie.

Ardent strawberry picker, connoisseur of
red ones and sneaker of greens.

Grinning golden haired wake-up-caller,
thrilled to find you where she hoped you'd be.

Foodie, sous-chef, aloft in her cooking tower;
specializing in whole wheat challah-kneading
and mixed-greens-tossing.

Wide-eyed listener/reader of 6 books at a sitting
with a few agains thrown in.

Extemporaneous choreographer
of organic dance forms, surprising even herself.

Squealing, swimming, sliding, giggling,
floating water being.

Joyful short-distance sprinter, greeting a friend
long missed since yesterday morning.

Focused artist of mixed media with penchants for both brush and finger.

Diligent plant waterer of unmatched reliability and frequency.

Heartfelt hugger and imparter of wet kisses with accompanying monologue of adoration.

Skilled dog coach, training Bro to both sleep on her bed and compete in equitation.

Enthusiastic jumper-up-and-down, wisechild, delighted that life is as it is.

MY LOVE'S NOSE

When you are gone from me
and a snorty nose honks in a crowd,
I'll search the source unflaggingly
and know it's you I'll find.

If a sneeze that wakes the dead
echoes through the Quarter,
I'll run and run to find it,
sure that you will be its author.

Transfusion

Cherry red vacuum packed
fresh organic blend
dangles overhead imbuing him
gota a gota with the promise
of a reprieve.

And it does pink him up,
restore comfort, wit, pleasure in
books and crosswords,
delicious expressions of love.

He returns to me and oddly
my grief intensifies.
My longing is constant, hard,
to capture this fresh time
in freeze frame.

I imagine this new blood
the pure beaten olive oil
of everlasting light,
burning long past its time.

I dream this new blood a hero's elixir
that balks and protests at the cancer
and says what the fuck is this doing here
and knocks it out. Eats it for lunch.

The doctor says its effects will last 2 weeks.
The dream is better.

HE'S LEAVING

He's leaving.
Most needs packed up.
No more names of food for choosing.

I stroke his head, his face, his skinny arms.
Sleep his only freedom now.

Now heavy breathing,
his damp hair in sweet curls
like our little Allie's.
I stroke his head, his arms,
kiss his face all over.
Unsure he can hear me, I say
I will love you forever, forever.

I leave the room briefly.
Return to pure quiet.
No breath, nor beat,
body still, face serene.
I kiss his lips 3 times.
They part slightly.

Between sobs, I'm a bit curious about the lips,
the faint smile.
Maybe there is life after death.
I gently snip some ringlets for keeping.
Goodbye my beautiful Joe, my precious guy.
I will love you forever, forever.

Orchids at 2100

You know exactly who you are
Struck silly by the sunlight that
Dazzled you as it did me that day
I decided we needed to live here

Ignorant of the natural order of things
Or in blatant disregard of it, you hold
Your precious blooms for illogical time
And then strike awe again in encore

The white speckled rose one that Jen sent
(Never been good with names)
Held full bloom for 10 months and then
Cavalierly sent up a flirtatious shoot
Just before the last flower fell

You oversized whites,
It should be sleight of hand that
Causes you to return more floriferous
And showy than when you first arrived
Having been tended by wiser hands than mine

While I struggle to "find myself,"
Define myself as my years advance,
You all must roll your misty eyes or at least
Giggle at the pursuit

Today I see so many new arrivals and
Way before you're due, I keep repeating
With each giddy discovery
You know exactly who you are
You know precisely what to do

A Green Death

I planted a Big Jim chile seed indoors
in a Santa Fe pot.
In two days the house was overrun
by a hoard of swarming gnats.

I placed a cup of red wine with sugar
on top of the soil, secure it would serve as bait.
Personally, I found it jaunty and herbaceous,
but would it satisfy the *culex pipiens*' taste?

They dove in like Kamikaze pilots.
Their numbers declined every day.
Their tiny bodies blanketed the surface—
something like death by gamay.

I now have a five-foot plant,
brimming with fruit in Jim's name.
Apropos of the gnats, I would love to know
if Temple Grandin finds that slaughter humane.

Unsure

As I face you and speak,
I'm looking past your eyes.

I don't want you to see the awkwardness
in my effort to seem wise.

I don't want to misuse or misapply a word,
or just go on ad libbing.

I want neither to snow you,
lest you think I'm narcissistic,
sound pitiful or, worse, boring;
still worse, masochistic.

If I appear too cynical or sarcastic,
I might read nihilistic.

I want to win your favor and approval but,
God forbid, sound needy.

I don't want to be an ass-kisser
or a take-you-or-leaver.

Sometimes it's easier to just be by myself.

If I can't read your preferences,
it's just too hard to guess.

BRO

He raised 2 babies—Alafair and Parker
His warm body cushioned their curly heads
His wet nose checked if they were okay and when not,
He lay beside them until they were
Mom taught them "gentle" astride his willing back
He taught them kindness through his tender ways,
His heavy paw landing light enough on their little arms,
His eyes expressing his bountiful love
Dear dear Bro, rest in peace
Take long walks with Papa and,
Snuggle up against him,
as you both watch over your family,
Who will remember and love you always
Our sweet beautiful Bro

I Watched You Dance Today

I watched you dance today
On the video on my iPad
Allie, Jen, and I were there
When you sambaed into the room
Your arms, hands, hips in synchrony
With the pulsing percussion
Of Rio's soundtrack
You and your sexy playful self
Jen belly laughing and filming
Allie not sure what was happening
I, giddy, so glad to see your surprise improv

I remembered in Acapulco
We asked the cab driver
Where he went to dance
And we went there and we danced for hours
And the guy from the other couple said
You dance like a fucking snake
We laughed our heads off

I decided I could see you dance today
It's almost two years now
I was afraid to fan that old feeling
Watch that easy sensual beauty of you
But today I saw you and I smiled and remembered
My sexy dancing guy

A Miracle

Legs collapsing, feet unaware of the
presence of shoes (not without looking),
bumping into walls here and there.
Both knees and shins icy cold in tandem;
flashes of heat next.
Ignorance trumps discovery, I'm still convinced.

A single prayer to Joe,
Come get me or let it be like
"The Princess and the Pea,"
one small thing causing calamitous consequences.
Shutting down by inches, from cane to walker,
to bed, until Jen challenges the absurd.

Revealing itself higher than imagined,
a bean (a loaner from the other fairy tale)
is perched on my spine. Jen hears "golf ball."
No matter sport or fable, the intruder advances,
Crushing mobility and now reason.

He finds it;
he, a cute brainy young Colombian MD.
Enlisting to thwart and expel the bean ball,
2 experts emerge. I focus on his name,
the one who leads the pair—Najeeb,
Arabic, I think; its meaning
"gracious, noble, intelligent."

And he saves the Jewish girl.
I give myself goosebumps.

My Jen comes, toting a bear tied
to a huge smiling balloon head.
Soon anthropomorphized, he lasts till today,
almost 2 months.
As he comes to his end,
he hangs out at diminishing altitudes,
Rising first, then, it seems, descending
to rest his head against Joe's
in the photo that faces me.

Today I walk solo around the block for the first time.
I think my 72-year-old gait kind of jaunty, no, cool.
I carry my cane like
a baton twirler cum drum majorette,
Giddy at the triumph that
it never touches the ground.

A miracle

No More Poems
(November 25, 2022, 5:26 p.m.)

Pain, you're slaying me
Uninvited body crasher
Breaking through security
Exploding who I am

You force me to dance
Against my will
You jerk me side to side
Till down is up and up is down

Then snatch my will as prize

No More Poems #2
(November 26, 2022, 10:56 a.m.)

Playing it close to the vest
Under cover of my walker
3 potted gardenias pocketed
I roll across the sod

The lust for planting dizzying
The scent of soil enticing
The feel of earth enraptures
The point of entry arises

An easy dig through richest soil
They're nestled in the ground
Back up the ramp stealth walker and I
Never sounding the alarm

About the Author

RONNIE BRENNER is a retired cognitive behavioral therapist (LCSW, BCD) who was in private practice for 24 years in her hometown of New Orleans. Prior to obtaining her MSW from Tulane University School of Social Work in 1990, she spent 18 years as the owner/director of Ronnie Brenner Fine Arts, showcasing original prints and drawings. Sharing her passion for the culinary arts, she spent several years cooking for families at Ronald McDonald House, and she continues to cultivate her love of feeding others by making dishes for family, neighbors, and friends. A passionate gardener—nicknamed "Ronnie Appleseed" by her husband for being known to wield clippers for deadheading wherever she goes—she delights in assisting friends and strangers with their gardens, and was once invited to show hers in the Garden District Association's Annual Garden Tour.

During the time of her beloved husband Joe's illness and subsequent passing in 2012, Ronnie was inspired to write the majority of the poems featured in this book. She now resides near her family in Petaluma, CA.

www.ingramcontent.com/pod-product-compliance
Lightning Source LLC
Chambersburg PA
CBHW021129080526
44587CB00012B/1207